summersdale

Summersdale Publishers Ltd
46 West Street
Chichester
West Sussex
PO19 1RP
UK

www.summersdale.com

Printed and bound in Great Britain

ISBN 1 84024 390 2

CONTENTS

INTRODUCTION

To do well at exams you have to be on your best form. This is obviously not possible if you're nervous, stressed and maybe even panicking, which will result in you not getting the results you deserve. But how can anyone be on their best form when the exam situation is so inherently stressful?

Passing exams is not just about knowing your subject. It's also about knowing yourself. It's about knowing how you react to stress, how you learn best, how to control your body's attempts to scare you away from the exam hall. If you understand your body and mind as well as your chosen subject then you have all the tools you need to perform to the best of your ability in the exam.

Much of this book is common sense. The tips aren't rocket science – they're the collective wisdom of generations of former students who know what it's like to suffer exam stress. Everybody works differently and responds in different ways to various stimuli, so it is important to understand yourself and use the tips that you think are most relevant for you. Above all, relax and do your best.

Revision

MAKE THE DECISION

The pass or fail decision is yours. It's up to you to show that you're capable of passing. The exam itself, the two or three hours in a large hall under the clock, is not where you pass or fail. By then, in many ways, it's too late. The work needed to pass starts well before the exam.

IMMERSE YOURSELF IN YOUR SUBJECT

If you live with a subject, immerse yourself in it daily for a long period, it becomes familiar and easy. Only the unfamiliar seems hard. Cover your walls with materials relating to the subject – lists, pictures, facts, charts, etc. Read about it first thing in the morning and mull it over at the bus stop, as well as during your regular revision hours. Remove the unfamiliarity and you remove the stress.

DON'T RUSH THINGS

Careful scheduling is everything. Prepare a revision timetable that is realistic and includes time to relax your mind. If you worry about achieving your revision goals then you're adding even more stress to the worry of the exams themselves.

The timetable must be one you can read clearly. You may even find it useful to mark your revision schedule in a Filofax-style diary.

CREATE A GOOD WORKING ENVIRONMENT

Before settling down to revision take the time to clear your desk, get all your materials in order and work out how you are going to tackle this study session. Make sure the room is free from distractions and have a cup of (decaffeinated) tea or a glass of water ready.

STOP...

... whenever you find your mind is wandering from the subject. Take a break, get some fresh air, stretch your muscles and come back to the revision with renewed energy.

HAVE SHORT STUDY SESSIONS

It's hard for the brain to concentrate for long without a break. Focus your learning time on half-hour sessions with five or ten minute breaks in between.

START EARLY ON

Long-term learning is better than short-term cramming. The brain responds better to amassing knowledge a little at a time over a long period. Trying to cram everything into a short period of revision time just adds to the stress and reduces the effectiveness of the learning.

SHARE YOUR LEARNING

Introduce a 'What did you learn today?' ritual with friends or family, whereby you give a synopsis of your day's learning in one or two sentences. This helps you retain the information and reminds you how interesting the subject is.

PLAN AHEAD

Your exams form a major landmark in your life. It's important to focus on them, so where possible try to avoid combining them with other major life events such as new babies, house moves, weddings, etc.

DO AS MANY MOCK EXAMS AS YOU CAN

Before each exam you should have already sat as many of the previous exams as possible in that subject by the same examination board for the last ten years. Hopefully you will have passed most of them and will be able to make a note of recurring themes and trends that will give you a clear indication of where to focus your revision time.

DO A MOCK EXAM JUST BEFORE THE REAL ONE

Going through the whole exam process a few days before the real thing gets you in tune with the subject and the concentration needed so that when you come to do it for real the experience is familiar and therefore less stressful.

DO A MOCK EXAM UNDER EXAM CONDITIONS

This works best away from the distractions of home: try setting yourself a mock exam in a library and go through the whole experience with no notes or cheating. But don't try this until you feel ready for it: the idea is to prepare yourself for the experience of an exam in order to reduce the stress of the real thing. Learn from the weaknesses this mock exam will inevitably expose.

TURN YOUR WEAKNESSES INTO STRENGTHS

Everyone has their weaknesses when it comes to exams. Don't overlook these problems: identify them and get your tutor to help you work at them until they become your strongest skills.

ASK QUESTIONS

Don't be afraid to ask questions in class – you may think all the other students are smarter than you but an inquisitive nature could well help you surpass their exam efforts.

DON'T IGNORE THE TOPICS YOU DON'T ENJOY

Within a subject there are usually aspects that are boring or harder work than others. Don't push these aside until the last minute – you'll be saving up stress for yourself.

SHARE YOUR PROBLEMS

If there is an aspect of a subject that you're having trouble grasping, don't keep your worries to yourself. Other students may have overcome similar obstacles as they climbed the learning curve and can help eliminate that particular cause of stress.

SHARE YOUR REVISION

Some students work better alone, others learn faster by revising with a partner and discussing the subject aloud. If you're not sure what works best for you make the time to experiment. Arrange a regular time to meet with another student and prepare for the study session by planning what you would like to work on with him/her.

SWAP NOTES

When you have completed a set of revision notes, swap them with the notes that someone on the same course has made in order to see if either of you has misunderstood something or missed a vital part of the topic altogether.

IDENTIFY YOUR FEARS

Sometimes students delay doing part of the revision until the thing they're ignoring becomes a stressful ogre in their minds. When you find you've been putting off revising a particular topic for no good reason, write down specifically what you are delaying and why. Usually the task isn't so hard to do as you originally thought.

USE COLOUR

When making revision notes,
prepare your materials in colour.
Using different colours to represent
different aspects of the subject will
help to lodge the concepts in your
brain more easily.

USE THE BRAINSTORM METHOD

Assess what you already know or have just revised by marking key words on a blank piece of paper and brainstorming associated facts, figures, names, etc. This will spark off inspiration and get the cogs of the brain turning.

USE MUSIC

Ever noticed how easy it is to learn song lyrics compared to prose? If you're feeling creative simply put your facts, quotes, lists or formulae to music, sing and record it, and play it back to yourself until you can sing it in your head word for word. You don't have to write an original tune; just put new words to your favourite songs.

USE MNEMONICS
AND RHYME

If hearing your own singing voice puts you off your breakfast, try turning your subject matter into rhyme or simple mnemonics to help those facts become easily accessible for your brain. For example, 'May I have a large container of coffee?' gives you the value of pi to seven decimal places (count the letters of each word).

DON'T LISTEN TO MUSIC...

... that you will want to sing along to. However, do play instrumental or classical music at an unobtrusively low volume if you find it helps block out other noise distractions. It will also help create a calming atmosphere in which to study.

KEEP YOUR NOTES BRIEF

Your revision notes shouldn't be long-winded. Key words should be enough to provide a link in your brain to the details you need. The whole purpose of taking notes is to distil whole textbooks into a few pages of easy-to-remember lists and summaries. It's far less stressful to read through some notes on a postcard before an exam than to be reading from a 500-page book.

READ ACTIVELY

Simply reading a chapter of a
textbook is not going to be sufficient
revision for that subject. A passive
read is fine for the first stage of
revision, just to familiarise yourself
with the subject, but active reading –
whereby you take notes as you read
and think about whether you really
understand everything – is the more
effective learning method.

TAKE A SUBJECT, DIVIDE AND DIVIDE AGAIN

A textbook is daunting to look at, heavy to carry and stress-inducing when you think about having to learn everything in it. The only way to master a whole exam subject is to break it down into manageable portions. Keep on subdividing it until you have something that can be summarised on a postcard that you can carry with you and look at frequently.

SUBDIVIDE
YOUR TIMETABLE

Smaller chunks of revision on your timetable can be completed more quickly. Get into the habit of ticking them off when done. The more things you tick off your list the more satisfaction you'll have that you're making progress and the greater will be the sense of momentum.

REVISE ONLY THE TOPICS YOU NEED TO

It's not an efficient use of your time to revise the entire course if you know that some aspects of it won't be tested or that you will have a choice of topics to answer questions on.

LOOK AT THE TREES, NOT THE FOREST

Even when you have timetabled only those topics that are necessary to learn and have subdivided those topics into manageable chunks it can still be daunting to look at the totality of the revision task that lies ahead. If you're worried about the exams then the size of the task will appear magnified and this will lead to stress. Avoid this by only thinking about one small topic at a time.

LOOK AT THE BRANCH, NOT THE TREE

In the same way that the entire process of months of revision is daunting, so is an individual day that is crammed with hours of difficult work. If you find yourself waking up, staring at the huge revision timetable on your wall and feeling stressed about the day's tasks, think in terms of just the first task of the day and look forward to tackling it successfully and ticking it off.

YOUR OWN NOTES ARE BEST

It's easy to get hold of pre-written notes and summaries for any academic subject. But it's not just about having a set of notes to carry around and learn: the actual process of making the notes in the first place is one of the best methods of learning the subject. If you skip that phase you're removing a vital part of your learning process which will only lead to a more stressful exam situation.

PERSONALISE
THE COURSE

The more you re-work and distil
the contents of the course into your
own words, the more meaningful it
becomes to you and the easier it will
be to remember everything.

STAY ACTIVE

Don't neglect your body while you're feeding your brain with facts. Build regular exercise or sport into your revision timetable and your mind will benefit from your body's fitness.

LEARN WITH
ALL YOUR SENSES

Don't just read or look at your computer. Find out if there are audiobooks, CDs or DVD/video dramatisations of the subject you're studying. Listen in the car, while you're walking or even while you're sleeping.

VARY YOUR TECHNIQUE

Stress can build up through the sheer monotony of working in the same way all the time. If you always revise in one particular way try new ways in order to keep your mind stimulated. Also vary your place of study if it helps to keep your enthusiasm up.

BUT DON'T CHANGE IT AT THE LAST MINUTE

In the final countdown to the exam itself changing your revision technique to a new one could be counterproductive. By all means keep rotating your learning systems so that you only use techniques that have already proven useful to you but don't experiment at the last minute and risk wasting that vital study time.

TEST YOURSELF

Once you have condensed a topic onto small cards it should be easy to learn by heart everything on that card. Keep them in your pocket and produce them regularly during the day to test yourself on their contents.

REWARD YOURSELF

Build some kind of reward into your revision timetable so that for each mini-session or topic covered you are able to take a break and do something you enjoy. Allow yourself to switch off your brain each day during your favourite TV soap opera, but only if you hit your revision targets first.

GET A JUMP START

If you're having trouble starting your revision, always putting it off and finding other things to do even though you've made a timetable, try reversing the situation: timetable the things you really want to do that have nothing to do with revision.
Do those things and tick them off, and in the gaps between them just revise.

Banish the stress

UNDERSTAND STRESS

Stress is the body's evolved reaction
to danger. It creates a change in a
person's biochemical balance that
enables a short-term enhancement
of strength and senses designed to
get that person either out of danger
quickly by running, or to help them
fight. Infrequent doses of stress
dissipate quickly, but regular
exposure to stress can
cause problems.

KEEP AN EYE ON STRESS

Stress is cumulative. Don't ignore minor worries about your exam. Stress can build up as multiple factors combine until you can't cope any more, so try to deal with every problem as it occurs so that the stress is always manageable. This also applies to stresses of everyday life – keep them under control and you'll find you can cope with your exams too.

EAT THE RIGHT THINGS

A balanced diet of natural and healthy foods will help your body to cope with stress more easily. Too much sugar or caffeine will exacerbate any feelings of stress you may have.

BUT ALSO EAT CHOCOLATE

Despite chocolate's high sugar content there are other ingredients that are known to have a calming effect.

DON'T CHANGE YOUR
DIET AT THE LAST MINUTE

Suddenly switching to a new kind of
diet, such as carbohydrate-free, just
a few days before the exam can
unnecessarily complicate your
body's ability to cope with stress.

GO TO BED

Make time to relax and feel tired the night before an exam. If you can get a good night's sleep your concentration levels will be improved.

BE PREPARED FOR BROKEN SLEEP

If you can't sleep well then don't fight it. Getting worked up about a sleepless night only makes it harder to sleep and leaves you more exhausted the next morning. It's normal to have broken sleep patterns during exam periods, so plan for this and try to find ways to minimise light and noise pollution in your bedroom to help you sleep. Drinking warm milk may help, too, as it is said that this reduces gastric secretion, influences stomach receptors and has a sedative effect.

DON'T CHEAT
YOUR BODY

You might think pills are a good way to calm the nerves, but they can impair concentration and slow your thinking. Drinking heavily the night before the exam in order to relax will also not help the next day. Your body needs to be fresh and alert, not drugged-up and dazed.

AVOID SMOKING

Some people smoke to alleviate stress, but it also increases blood pressure and can add to feelings of anxiety.

DON'T FOCUS ON FINANCE

The combination of being in debt and feeling the pressure of looming exams is a common cause of stress for students. It's no good telling yourself that if you pass the exam you can get a good job and pay off those debts, because that adds to the pre-exam pressure. And worrying too much about the lack of money will hinder your exam performance. There's no simple solution. All you can attempt to do is to become a stronger, more capable individual who can take these problems in their stride and use the de-stress techniques to cope on a day-to-day basis. But talk to others about your problems, both friends and counsellors.

TALK ABOUT
RELATIONSHIP PROBLEMS

These problems can crop up at any time, and if there's a break-up just before your exams it's inevitably going to add to your stress. Saving your relationship under these circumstances is sadly beyond the scope of this book. As with financial worries, the best positive advice is to use the de-stress techniques to become a stronger person who can shoulder the burden of these problems. It will also help to talk about your situation with friends and student counsellors.

BELIEVE IN YOURSELF

You can do it. You've worked hard for this. You know your subject. Take pleasure in the thought of showing off your knowledge to a cynical examiner.

RATIONALISE

You already qualified to get on this course in the first place, and you wouldn't have been accepted if it wasn't thought that you were capable of passing.

DON'T UNDERRATE YOUR PAST ACHIEVEMENTS

If you convince yourself that any previous exam success was undeserved or a fluke then you're going to have extra cause for concern about your potential this time around. Tell yourself that your previous passes were fully earned and that you obviously have what it takes.

DON'T COMPARE YOURSELF WITH OTHERS

Remember, everyone has strengths *and* weaknesses, but usually in different areas. Measuring yourself up against other students can never be accurate or the least bit productive.

SET REALISTIC GOALS

Aiming too far beyond your capability
is going to cause stress. Set a goal of
improving your grades by one level
rather than jumping from bottom
of the class to top of the class
in one year.

TAKE TIME
OFF FROM REVISING

Your timetable should not use every
available day for revision. Build in a
small number of days where your
brain is rested and you can have
some guilt-free fun.

TAKE TIME
OFF FROM WORK

If you're balancing exams with a job,
try to get time off a few days before
the exam so that you can focus your
mind on just the exam.

KNOW WHERE THE EXAM IS TAKING PLACE

Don't rely on simply knowing where the building is: which part of the building will you need to find on the day? If you've not been there before you can eliminate unnecessary last-minute stress by making sure you know where to park, where to wait before the exam, where the toilets are, etc.

KNOW WHEN THE EXAM IS TAKING PLACE

Exam timetables or notices tell you when the exam actually starts but you will be expected to get to the exam hall some time earlier or you may not be let in. Find out what how much earlier you need to be there and arrive a few minutes ahead of that time.

MEDITATE

Find five minutes a day in your revision plan to sit in a quiet place, close your eyes, and let your mind take you to a beach where the waves are lapping at your toes and the sun is warming your body.

RELAX YOUR MUSCLES

Muscle tension caused by stress can be alleviated by exercise and by the simple technique of tensing your whole body and then relaxing the muscles and feeling the stress flowing out of you as you do so.

WIND DOWN
EVERY NIGHT

After a hard day's work it's important
to have some time to wind down.
You should have punctuated your day
with short breaks, but if the looming
exam leaves you anxious last thing at
night try to wind down with a hot
bath or some soothing music.

The day of the exam

TAKE A SHOWER

You need to feel fresh and awake and this is the best way to start the day.

EAT SOMETHING

You might feel too nervous to eat a good breakfast, but getting some food inside you will help your concentration.

RELY ON SLEEP, NOT CAFFEINE

Many students take energy drinks and tablets to compensate for lack of sleep. But high caffeine doses won't give you the same mental awareness as a good night's sleep. If you revise through the night and rely on stimulants to stop you falling asleep during the exam you'll find your thinking is cloudy.

AVOID ALCOHOL

Alcohol will make you feel relaxed but it also impairs memory, so you don't want to be taking a swig from a hip-flask just before the exam.

HAVE A
POSITIVE ATTITUDE

Start the day with a positive mental approach. Tell yourself this is going to be the day that you pass your exam and look forward to the celebrations when the results come through. Make sure you also have a treat planned for after the exam.

REHEARSE IN YOUR HEAD

Take a moment to sit and go through
some likely scenarios in your head.
Visualise turning over the test paper
and reading the questions
with confidence.

WEAR A WATCH

You don't want to be late. That would only add to your stress. Make sure the watch is accurate. Some people find it helpful to remove their watch in the exam hall and place it on the desk to help time their essay writing (even though all exam halls have clocks!).

CHECK YOUR STATIONERY SUPPLIES

Make sure you have more than enough pens and other stationery items to last the duration of the exam. Also check that what you are bringing is permitted within the rules. If a calculator is allowed do you have a spare battery (or even a spare calculator)?

FIND A HIGH-SPEED PEN

You need to write fast in exams and the speed of the pen might be a factor in whether you have time to put all of your relevant knowledge into your answer. Cheap biros might be slower than rollerballs or other pen types. Experiment with a few brands until you find one that works well for your handwriting style.

RELISH THE NERVES

Being a little nervous puts your body
in a slightly hyper state, fuelled by
adrenalin that heightens your
concentration and performance.
Don't be scared of the feeling –
harness and use it to your advantage.

THINK AHEAD

One day you will have passed this exam. You might even go on to study the same subject at higher levels and you'll look back on this day and wonder what all the fuss was about. Try to visualise yourself with that future level of confidence and retain it as you enter the exam hall.

GET THINGS IN PERSPECTIVE

As well as visualising your fully qualified future try to look at the rest of your life in perspective. Is this exam going to be so relevant one day when you have a job and a family?

TALK TO YOUR DOCTOR

For people with a history of stress and anxiety in exams it's possible for your doctor to prescribe beta-blockers to remove the symptoms and help you feel more calm and in control. Talk to your doctor if anxiety is going to be a real concern for you.

MAKE THE MOST OF YOUR SHORT-TERM MEMORY

Many students prefer not to do last-minute revision as they stand outside the exam hall waiting to go in, but we all have a capacity for short-term memory that should be used at this time. You could easily upload ten new facts into your head just before you enter the hall, then write those facts down just five minutes later as soon as you're allowed to pick up your pens. Write them down before you even look at the questions and you'll have one extra resource to turn to.

VISUALISE SUCCESS

Experiments have shown that students who visualise themselves succeeding are more likely to succeed than those who don't, and yet most students spend their time pessimistically visualising failure.

Exam technique

READ ALL THE
INSTRUCTIONS FIRST

It's a common requirement that only a certain number of questions from certain sections need be answered. Don't assume that the requirements will be the same as in the past papers you studied: read the instructions carefully and make sure you understand them because they might have changed since the previous year.

READ ALL THE QUESTIONS FIRST

If you have a choice of questions it's essential to read all of them and note which ones you think would give you the optimum opportunity for showing off your knowledge. Don't rush when deciding which ones to answer.

READ EACH QUESTION CAREFULLY

Examiners take great care in the wording of questions. The usage of the words is deliberate and sometimes it's intended to catch out unwary students. Read it carefully and make sure your answer is relevant. There's nothing more stressful than getting to the end of a long essay only to glance back at the question and realise you've misread it.

MAKE A TIMETABLE

Exams can last as long as three hours or more, and it sounds like such a long time that students commonly spend too long on the first questions and have to rush through the final ones in a state of stressed panic. So when you've chosen your questions make a timetable so that you know how long you have to answer each one. If possible, allow some minutes at the end to review your work.

REVISE YOUR TIMETABLE

If you find yourself over-running in one part of the exam, revise your timetable so that the remaining time is split evenly between the other questions. This ensures that you can at least partially answer all questions.

DON'T PANIC IF YOU RUN OUT OF TIME

Anticipate the end of the exam so that even if you are halfway through an essay you can at least spend the last couple of minutes scribbling notes about what you would have written had you had more time. Credit is sometimes given for notes even when the question isn't fully answered.

ANSWER EASY
QUESTIONS FIRST

Give your morale a leg-up by tackling
the questions you feel most confident
about before trying the difficult ones.
At least you'll have some good
answers under your belt before
taking on something you're
less sure of.

ANSWER THE REQUIRED NUMBER OF QUESTIONS

In a four essay paper, four essays written moderately well might score higher than three essays written so brilliantly that there wasn't time for a fourth.

DON'T GIVE UP

If you think you've made a mistake that will result in failure, don't give up. Fix it fast, amend your answer, or move on to other questions. It's always possible that you might pass despite failing a small part of the exam.

AIM FOR COMPETENCE NOT PERFECTION

The examiner is looking for sufficient evidence that you are competent in your chosen subject. You don't have to be perfect. No one can hold all the knowledge of a subject in their heads, not even the examiner.

TALK TO YOURSELF (SILENTLY)

If you feel that stress and anxiety are building up inside you, have a strong word with yourself. Remind yourself of all the hard work that has gone into preparing for this exam and tell yourself to revel in showing off all that knowledge to the examiner.

DON'T WORRY
ABOUT A MENTAL BLANK

This is normal. Under exam pressure or due to lack of sleep the night before students often stare at a question to which they would normally be able to come up with a passable answer and find they cannot make any sense of it. It's OK. Don't waste more than a couple of minutes trying to find the information that you know you filed somewhere in your head but seem to have mislaid. Go on to another question and come back to this one later. In the majority of cases the mental blank will have cleared just by ignoring the problem and thinking about something else.

WORK AROUND
A MENTAL BLANK

If you come back to this problem question (or if it's the last question and there's nothing else to go to) try breaking it down into component parts. Make some notes. Rewrite the question in your own words. Think laterally about the issues you think the examiner is interested in with this question. Tackle the problem from a new perspective until you find your answer begins to flow.

USE YOUR REVISION TECHNIQUE IN THE EXAM

Your revision technique of making notes, lists and linked ideas from the original source material will apply equally well in the exam. Make notes about the question from the information that is in your head and use those notes when formulating your answer.

LABEL YOUR
WORK CLEARLY

There's no point in being a genius if the exam paper can't be attributed to you. Make sure your name and any reference numbers are clearly written on each page in the appropriate place.

When panic strikes during the exam

CLOSE YOUR EYES

Take a few seconds to remove the
visual stimuli that are contributing to
the feeling of stress: the ticking clock,
the rows of desks, the tutors, the
exam paper and the good luck
charms on your desk. Clear them
from your head and prepare your
mind to face them with strength.

BREATHE SLOWLY

Breathe in deeply, hold for a second, then breathe out slowly. Repeat three times, concentrating on nothing else. This technique sets the mind free from distractions and worries and calms your heart rate.

AVOID
HYPERVENTILATING

If you find yourself breathing with rapid, shallow breaths that seem out of control you could be hyperventilating. Remedy this by trying to hold your breath after each exhalation for just a second or two, or by breathing into a small paper bag (bring one with you if you think you might need it).

BRAINWASH YOURSELF

Take control of your mind. Chant simple, positive mantras in your head that will kick out the feeling of panic and restore mental law and order. Repeat these positive phrases (things like 'I will succeed', 'I am in control', etc.) until your head has been 'washed' of all its negativity.

COUNT SHEEP

Or anything else you can see out of the window. Count backwards from ten. Count the other students in the hall. Just take the focus of your thoughts away from the exam that's causing your stress until you regain control and feel able to face the exam once more.

TRY A
DIFFERENT QUESTION

If your panic leads to you staring at the question paper until the words become meaningless shapes and you can't understand the question, try the simple breathing technique and then move to a different question. If this happens at the start of the exam, don't worry – it's common for stress levels to be highest at the very start. Calm yourself, focus and breathe and your stress levels will quickly reduce.

THINK OF THE WORST CASE SCENARIO

What is the worst that can happen if you fail? Is it the end of the world? Have others failed this exam before you and still gone on to have happy, productive lives? Put your fears into perspective, accept whatever the worst can be and know that every extra bit of effort you put into your exam will result in something a little better than the worst result.

IF ALL ELSE FAILS
TELL THE EXAMINER

The examiners aren't just there to make you feel intimidated – they can also help. If the feeling of panic is overwhelming and nothing you try makes things improve then tell an examiner so they can accompany you outside and help you to calm down.

After the exam

TREAT YOURSELF

Congratulate yourself. Don't dwell
on what you might have done badly.
You went through a difficult and
stressful situation and it's over now.
You can have that drink that you really
wanted before the exam started!

REVIEW YOUR PERFORMANCE

You can chat to other students after the exam to see how they reacted to the questions, but if this process makes you feel vulnerable and inadequate then don't bother. Just think objectively about how well prepared you were and whether there are any lessons to be learned that would help your future exams.

Why people fail

NOT BEING READY

Some people take the exam hoping for a fluke, knowing their knowledge is not really good enough to guarantee a pass. This usually results in failure.

OVERWHELMED BY STRESS

When stress can't be controlled it leads to panic. In that state of mind students perform very poorly. They can't think straight, can't concentrate, can't function. Often this happens to people who get good grades for coursework but who cannot cope with the pressure of the exam environment.

OVERWHELMED
BY PRESSURE

Students often think more about the significance the exam has to their future lives and careers than they do about the mechanics of actually passing it. If the exam is crucial to qualify in a chosen career then the sense of pressure can distract from the need to get on and revise for it.

OVERCONFIDENCE

Eliminating all signs of exam-related stress is generally a good thing, but if it makes you too confident of your skills or in denial of the reality of your state of preparedness then it can have a negative effect. Balance your confidence with respect for the subject matter and for the examiner.

FAILURE TO STICK TO THE REVISION TIMETABLE

There is only a finite time available in which to revise. Your revision timetable should have covered all the necessary syllabus topics, but students fail when they try to be perfectionists, refusing to move on from one topic until they are a world authority on it. This results in being a genius at a small part of the syllabus and knowing nothing about the rest.

PRE-ASSUMPTION OF FAILURE

Pessimistic students do themselves no favours by assuming they will fail before they have even completed their revision period. This negative attitude taints their whole revision process, with a subconscious feeling that there's no point in revising because they won't pass anyway. Tackle this by accepting that perhaps part of the exam will be failed but focusing on aspects that are stronger so that there is still a chance of passing overall.

More help

SPECIAL CONSIDERATION

If your personal circumstances prior to the exams change beyond your control such that you are unable to focus on your revision and the exams themselves, it may be worth visiting your student counsellor. In some cases it might be possible to delay the exams to give you time to get over your personal problems.

The Samaritans
Telephone 08457 90 90 90 or visit
their website: www.samaritans.org.

The Student Counselling Service
Visit their website to find the contact
details for your college:
www.studentcounselling.org.

ChildLine
Younger exam takers can call
ChildLine on 0800 1111 or visit their
website: www.childline.org.uk.

DRIVING TEST TIPS

summersdale *self-help*